CW00601632

LET'S START SHORE *FISHING*

Richard Willett

The Crowood Press

First published in 1990 by
The Crowood Press
Ramsbury, Marlborough,
Wiltshire SN8 2HE

© The Crowood Press 1990

All rights reserved. No part of this publication may be
reproduced or transmitted in any form or by any
means, electronic or mechanical, including
photocopy, recording, or any information storage and
retrieval system without permission in writing from
the publishers.

British Library Cataloguing in Publication Data

Willett, Richard
    Shore fishing.
    1. Coastal waters. Shore angling. Manuals
    I. Title
    799.1'6

    ISBN 0–232–51857–2

Typeset by Jahweh Associates, Stroud
Printed in Great Britain by MacLehose & Partners Ltd

Contents

Flounder

Surf beaches and shingle banks provide good flounder fishing throughout the course of the year. You can expect to hook flounder on most bottom-fished rigs and baits. They are a fish that is likely to turn up no matter what you are fishing for.

Between December and early March, flounder concentrate in the lower reaches of major river systems and in minor estuaries and salt-water inlets.

Flounder accept most meaty baits and lugworms; ragworms, fish, sandeels and crabs are all snapped up. Peeler and soft crabs head the list of specialist flounder baits, followed by lively sandeels and fresh herring strips. White and harbour ragworms are extremely good baits but if all fails, lug and mackerel do well enough.

Two- and three-hook paternosters are excellent for general bottom fishing and also permit hard casting if needed. Flounder are mainly hooked at short to medium range but there are times when distance is needed and you may need to keep in touch with a creek or gulley as the tide forces you back up the beach.

Short snoods tied direct to stand-off loops are spaced 18 inches apart along the centre rib of the paternoster. Nine-

peeler crab

flounder hooked

inch snoods of 15-pound line are adequate. No flounder can break even 6-pound line on a direct pull but the fish's sharp teeth grind the line just above the hook.

Small fine-wire hooks are the answer. Blue Aberdeens in the size 2–2/0 are big enough to hold the bait and land big fish – even cod. The wire is also soft and pliable. Hold the fish across its back, pull on the trace until you feel the hook straighten, then smoothly increase pressure until the hook pulls free of the fish. This may sound a bit brutal but in this case it is much kinder than using forceps.

Sinker weight depends on the fishing ground. Calm water and modest tides allow 1- to 2-ounce rigs. As a rule you can fish 4 to 6 ounces of lead with ease from most estuary banks and beaches.

If the flounders are running and feeding hard, simply cast out and wait for a bite. At the height of the season you can afford to leave the first fish out there, while another flounder attacks the second hook. The bites are both positive and powerful and the flounder hook themselves against the force of the sinker.

Today's conservation-minded anglers protect their catch by placing them in a bucket of fresh sea water. If kept away from the sun they will live to fight another day.

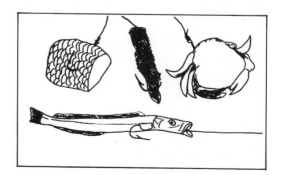

Bass

All around the southern coastline of Britain, beaches of boulders and tide pools are flooded at high tide and exposed as the water ebbs. Some are backed by cliffs, others by shingle banks. All are interlaced with channels and gulleys which thread between the weeds and stones that shelter crabs and elvers and shellfish.

From late April to October there are no better places to fish for shore bass. Bass move in when the tide floods, swimming through the weeds and shallow water in search of food.

At low tide, survey the area and collect the bait at the same time. Peelers and jelly-soft crabs are the best baits for bass, though tide-pool crab collecting is hard on the hands. Use a glove to reach down into the water. Store your crabs in wet weed. Use a deep bucket kept in the shade or, better still, cover it with a damp cloth.

Start fishing at dead low water. Very often some big bass are hooked on the lower beach.

A light to medium shore-casting rod light enough to hold all day and balanced to 2 to 4 ounces of lead is the best for bite detection. Here on the rocks a 40-yard cast is often routine. Set up with a fast multiplier or fixed spool reel. You must have sufficient speed to lift the tackle up and into clear water.

store these
in a
bucket

Cod

1. Shore anglers catch cod from a variety of different beaches.
2. The essential features of an open-water cod beach lie beneath the surface so make a point of surveying your local beach at low tide. Look for gulleys, depressions, stones and weed patches.
3. Semi-darkness, vicious tidal currents and churning waves boost a cod's confidence and expose food creatures.

sandbank

4. Cod move in and out breaks in sandbanks, hence a need for a good look at your local beach to find these hot spots.

5. Where the beach shelves down onto hard-packed sand and mud, cod swim along for considerable distances. The exact location of bait is less critical.

6. Even so, hot spots must still be found. Look for deeper water and a swirl of tide; these hold food and fish.

7. If you aim to catch cod regularly, it is a good idea to go night fishing with a friend.

Mackerel

1. Mackerel shoals drive baitfish right into the surf; on calm summer days you can actually hear them feeding.

2. Toss in a spinner or feathers. Let this sink, retrieve and the shoal will attack instantly.

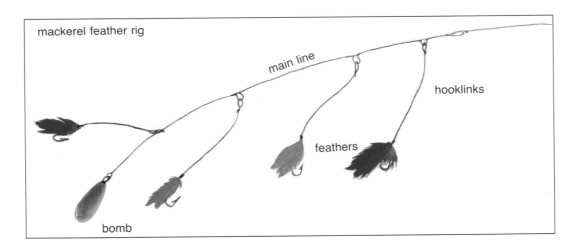

mackerel feather rig

main line

hooklinks

feathers

bomb

mackerel chasing feathers

3. For most species of sea fish mackerel is the main bait to use. A beachcaster rigged with a string of feathers can pull out five or six fish at a time.

4. Minimum casting weight plus a quick retrieve will keep the feathers in the surface layers.

5. Cast out, and then work the feathers back briskly in a sink and draw motion.

6. Two ways of finding mackerel are to scan the sea with binoculars and to watch gulls follow the mackerel in order to feed on them.

Thornback Rays

rays

rays

tideline

beach

a hidden ray

1. When spring warms the inshore waters masses of thornback rays invade the beaches of the west coast, the Channel and North Sea banks and the bigger estuary systems.
2. Rays shovel themselves into the sand so that only their eyes and spiracles are exposed.
3. The key to successful angling is to identify the holding grounds. On an open beach the majority of rays are probably hooked in two or three sections of the shore.
4. Estuaries and their offshore sand-banks are a definite draw to rays.

5. Average sizes of shore-caught rays range from five to twelve pounds.
6. Good baits are: whole peeler crabs, live 6-inch sandeels, king ragworm and a section of meat and guts from a mackerel.

7. Hooks should be strong stainless steel with a needle-sharp point.
8. Rays flop over the bait so use a long trace (20 to 30 inches) of 20- to 30-pound nylon to prevent the wings from fouling the line.

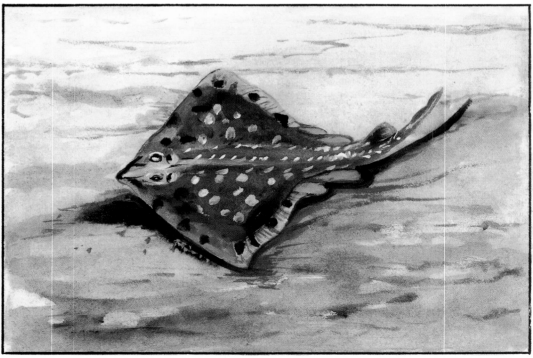

Wrasse

1.   Wrasse bite and dive, with the bite varying between a tremor which hardly moves the line and a powerful dash which sinks the float into a whirlpool of water.

2.   Watch for a definite movement of the float, then count to three slowly as you lower the rod tip and take up the slack line.

3.   When you lift, the rod arc is sufficient to hold the fish and bring its head up.

4.   Most wrasse can be lifted out by the rod or hand-lined up the rocks.

5.   Sometimes it is even necessary to lift the fish outwards from the rock face; this is where a long rod of 11 or 12 feet will offer more direct control.

6.   Invest in a good-quality pair of long-nosed forceps for unhooking; wrasse are quite capable of crunching the odd finger.

7.   Handle them carefully and return them to the sea.

hooking a wrasse

Conger Eels

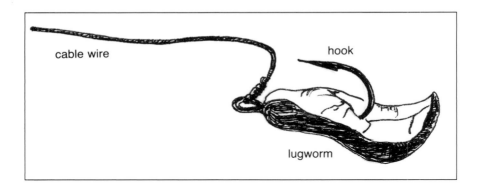

cable wire

hook

lugworm

1. Conger terminal tackle: 4–6/0 Seamaster or O'Shaughnessy hook, 18 inches of cable-laid wire of 100-pound breaking strain, or 80- to 130-pound monofilament.

2. Cast into the rough ground, set the reel in free spool, click the ratchet on and wait for a conger to steal the bait.
3. Keep your eyes glued to the tip ring. Congers bite very gently.

5.   Another foot of line comes up the rod ring – he's off with the bait.
6.   Push the reel into gear, switch off the ratchet, point the rod at the fish and reel in some slack line.
7.   When you feel the fish's weight, lift as hard and as high as possible.
8.   Drop nets are a real help as the conger will lie still as you unhook it. Then put it back.

4.   When 2 or 3 inches of line creep from the reel . . . wait, give it time to make off with the bait.

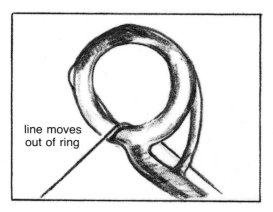

line moves
out of ring

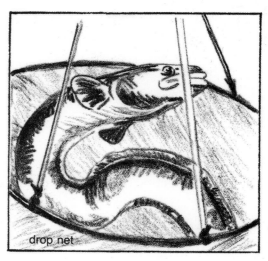

drop net

Rigs

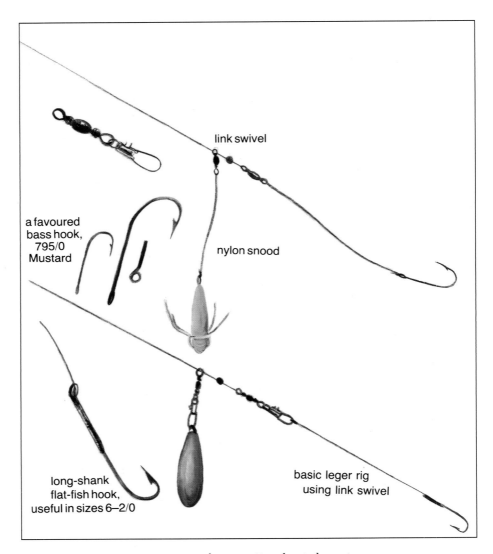

link swivel

a favoured
bass hook,
795/0
Mustard

nylon snood

long-shank
flat-fish hook,
useful in sizes 6–2/0

basic leger rig
using link swivel

*Basic running leger rig. Barrel swivel running
on nylon leader. This system incorporates a
short nylon lead dropper, suitable when using a
grip lead. Use a link swivel.*

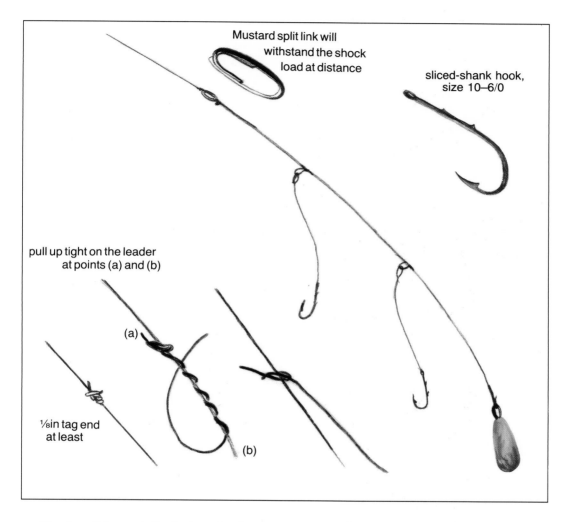

Mustard split link will
withstand the shock
load at distance

sliced-shank hook,
size 10–6/0

pull up tight on the leader
at points (a) and (b)

(a)

⅛in tag end
at least

(b)

The shore fisherman's Leader knot. Used to attach a casting leader of heavy-gauge nylon to the reel.

Basic nylon paternoster rig. 4ft in length from lead to reel line connection, forming the same breaking strain as casting leader.

Knots

Three-turn Loop knot.

Method of joining hook length to reel line.

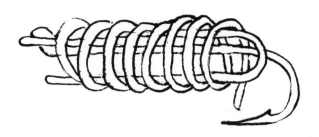

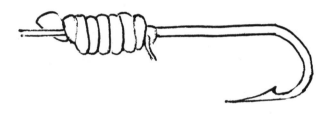

Spade End knot.

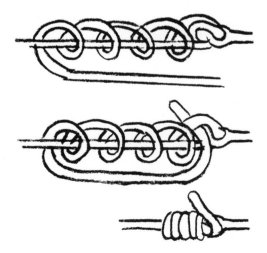

Clinch knot.

Index